50 Wild Game Cooking Recipes for Home

By: Kelly Johnson

Table of Contents

- Grilled Venison Steaks
- Elk Burger with Caramelized Onions
- Roasted Wild Boar Ribs
- Rabbit Stew with Vegetables
- Baked Pheasant with Garlic and Herbs
- Venison Chili
- Pan-Seared Quail with Mushroom Sauce
- Wild Turkey Tacos
- Smoked Duck Breast
- Elk and Mushroom Stroganoff
- Roasted Goose with Apples
- Venison Meatballs in Marinara Sauce
- Pheasant Pot Pie
- Grilled Bison Burgers
- Braised Rabbit with Mustard Sauce
- Wild Game Sausage
- Venison Jerky
- Slow Cooker Wild Game Stew
- Quail with Blackberry Glaze
- Elk Fajitas
- Stuffed Pheasant Breast
- Wild Mushroom and Venison Risotto
- Herb-Crusted Wild Boar Tenderloin
- Rabbit Cacciatore
- Grilled Duck Legs with Honey Glaze
- Venison Shepherd's Pie
- Pan-Fried Quail with Country Gravy
- Wild Game Jambalaya
- Bison Meatloaf
- Smoked Venison Tenderloin
- Duck Confit
- Elk and Sweet Potato Hash
- Grilled Wild Game Skewers
- Venison and Black Bean Chili
- Baked Pheasant with Cranberries

- Rabbit Fricassée
- Wild Turkey Breast with Sage Butter
- Venison Stroganoff with Egg Noodles
- Grilled Bison Steak with Chimichurri
- Roasted Wild Duck with Orange Sauce
- Venison Fajitas with Peppers
- Spicy Wild Boar Chili
- Braised Elk Shanks
- Pheasant Enchiladas
- Duck Breast with Cherry Sauce
- Venison Ragu with Pasta
- Grilled Quail with Lemon and Thyme
- Elk Meatballs with Cranberry Sauce
- Stuffed Rabbit Loin
- Wild Game Curry

Grilled Venison Steaks
Ingredients:

- 2 venison steaks
- 2 tablespoons olive oil
- 2 cloves garlic (minced)
- Salt and pepper to taste
- Fresh rosemary or thyme (optional)

Instructions:

1. **Prepare Marinade:** In a bowl, mix olive oil, minced garlic, salt, pepper, and herbs if using.
2. **Marinate Steaks:** Coat the venison steaks in the marinade and let them sit for at least 30 minutes at room temperature.
3. **Preheat Grill:** Preheat the grill to medium-high heat.
4. **Grill Steaks:** Place steaks on the grill and cook for 4-5 minutes on each side for medium-rare, adjusting time based on thickness.
5. **Serve:** Remove from grill and let rest for a few minutes before slicing and serving.

Elk Burger with Caramelized Onions
Ingredients:

- 1 pound ground elk meat
- 1 teaspoon garlic powder
- Salt and pepper to taste
- 2 onions (sliced)
- 2 tablespoons butter
- Burger buns
- Optional toppings: cheese, lettuce, tomato, pickles
  Instructions:
1. **Caramelize Onions:** In a skillet, melt butter over medium heat. Add sliced onions and cook slowly, stirring occasionally, until golden brown (about 15-20 minutes).
2. **Prepare Patties:** In a bowl, combine ground elk meat, garlic powder, salt, and pepper. Form into burger patties.
3. **Cook Burgers:** In another skillet or grill, cook the patties over medium-high heat for 4-5 minutes per side or until cooked through.
4. **Assemble Burgers:** Serve the elk patties on buns topped with caramelized onions and any additional toppings.

Roasted Wild Boar Ribs
Ingredients:

- 2 pounds wild boar ribs
- 2 tablespoons olive oil
- 1 teaspoon smoked paprika
- 1 teaspoon garlic powder
- Salt and pepper to taste
- 1 cup barbecue sauce

Instructions:

1. **Preheat Oven:** Preheat the oven to 300°F (150°C).
2. **Prepare Ribs:** In a bowl, mix olive oil, smoked paprika, garlic powder, salt, and pepper. Rub this mixture all over the ribs.
3. **Roast Ribs:** Place ribs on a baking sheet and cover with foil. Roast in the oven for 2-3 hours until tender.
4. **Add Sauce:** Remove the foil, brush with barbecue sauce, and bake for an additional 30 minutes uncovered to caramelize.
5. **Serve:** Slice between the ribs and serve with extra barbecue sauce.

Rabbit Stew with Vegetables
Ingredients:

- 1 rabbit (cut into pieces)
- 2 tablespoons olive oil
- 1 onion (chopped)
- 2 carrots (sliced)
- 2 celery stalks (sliced)
- 3 cloves garlic (minced)
- 4 cups chicken or vegetable broth
- 1 bay leaf
- Salt and pepper to taste
- Fresh thyme (optional)

Instructions:

1. **Sear Rabbit:** In a large pot, heat olive oil over medium heat. Add rabbit pieces and brown on all sides.
2. **Sauté Vegetables:** Remove rabbit and add onion, carrots, and celery to the pot. Cook until softened, then add garlic and cook for another minute.
3. **Add Rabbit and Broth:** Return rabbit to the pot, add broth, bay leaf, thyme, salt, and pepper.
4. **Simmer:** Bring to a boil, then reduce heat and simmer for 1.5 to 2 hours until rabbit is tender.
5. **Serve:** Remove bay leaf and serve warm with crusty bread.

Baked Pheasant with Garlic and Herbs
Ingredients:

- 2 pheasant breasts
- 2 tablespoons olive oil
- 4 cloves garlic (minced)
- 1 teaspoon dried thyme
- 1 teaspoon dried rosemary
- Salt and pepper to taste
- Lemon wedges (for serving)

Instructions:

1. **Preheat Oven:** Preheat the oven to 375°F (190°C).
2. **Prepare Marinade:** In a bowl, mix olive oil, garlic, thyme, rosemary, salt, and pepper.
3. **Marinate Pheasant:** Coat the pheasant breasts in the marinade and let sit for 15-30 minutes.
4. **Bake:** Place breasts in a baking dish and bake for 25-30 minutes until cooked through.
5. **Serve:** Serve with lemon wedges for added flavor.

Venison Chili

Ingredients:

- 1 pound ground venison
- 1 onion (chopped)
- 2 cloves garlic (minced)
- 1 can (15 oz) kidney beans (drained and rinsed)
- 1 can (15 oz) diced tomatoes
- 1 tablespoon chili powder
- 1 teaspoon cumin
- Salt and pepper to taste

Instructions:

1. **Cook Venison:** In a large pot, cook ground venison over medium heat until browned. Drain excess fat.
2. **Sauté Vegetables:** Add onion and garlic; cook until softened.
3. **Add Remaining Ingredients:** Stir in kidney beans, diced tomatoes, chili powder, cumin, salt, and pepper.
4. **Simmer:** Reduce heat and let simmer for 30-45 minutes.
5. **Serve:** Serve hot with your choice of toppings like cheese or sour cream.

Pan-Seared Quail with Mushroom Sauce
Ingredients:

- 4 quail (cleaned and prepared)
- Salt and pepper to taste
- 2 tablespoons olive oil
- 1 cup mushrooms (sliced)
- 1 cup chicken broth
- 2 tablespoons heavy cream

Instructions:

1. **Season Quail:** Season quail with salt and pepper.
2. **Sear Quail:** Heat olive oil in a skillet over medium-high heat. Add quail and sear on each side for 3-4 minutes until cooked through. Remove and set aside.
3. **Cook Mushrooms:** In the same skillet, add mushrooms and sauté until tender.
4. **Add Broth and Cream:** Pour in chicken broth and bring to a simmer. Stir in heavy cream and return quail to the skillet to warm through.
5. **Serve:** Serve quail with mushroom sauce drizzled over the top.

Wild Turkey Tacos
Ingredients:

- 1 pound ground wild turkey
- 1 onion (chopped)
- 2 cloves garlic (minced)
- 1 packet taco seasoning
- Taco shells
- Optional toppings: lettuce, cheese, salsa

Instructions:

1. **Cook Turkey:** In a skillet, sauté onion and garlic until softened. Add ground turkey and cook until browned.
2. **Add Seasoning:** Stir in taco seasoning and a little water; simmer for 5 minutes.
3. **Assemble Tacos:** Fill taco shells with turkey mixture and top with desired toppings.
4. **Serve:** Serve immediately.

Smoked Duck Breast
Ingredients:

- 2 duck breasts
- Salt and pepper to taste
- 1 tablespoon smoked paprika
- Optional: Cherry or apple wood chips for smoking
  Instructions:
1. **Prepare Duck:** Score the skin of the duck breasts and season with salt, pepper, and smoked paprika.
2. **Smoke:** Preheat smoker to 225°F (107°C). Place duck breasts skin side up on the grill grate. Smoke for about 1.5 hours.
3. **Sear:** Increase heat to 400°F (204°C) and sear breasts skin side down for 5-7 minutes until crispy.
4. **Serve:** Slice and serve warm.

Elk and Mushroom Stroganoff
Ingredients:

- 1 pound elk steak (sliced thin)
- 1 onion (chopped)
- 2 cups mushrooms (sliced)
- 2 cloves garlic (minced)
- 1 cup beef broth
- 1 cup sour cream
- 1 tablespoon flour
- Salt and pepper to taste
- Egg noodles (for serving)

Instructions:

1. **Cook Elk:** In a skillet, sauté elk slices until browned; remove from skillet.
2. **Sauté Vegetables:** In the same skillet, add onion, mushrooms, and garlic; cook until softened.
3. **Make Sauce:** Stir in flour, then add beef broth and bring to a simmer. Return elk to the skillet and simmer for 10 minutes.
4. **Finish with Sour Cream:** Stir in sour cream and season with salt and pepper.
5. **Serve:** Serve over cooked egg noodles.

Roasted Goose with Apples
Ingredients:

- 1 whole goose (about 10-12 pounds)
- 4 apples (quartered)
- 1 onion (quartered)
- 2 tablespoons olive oil
- 1 teaspoon salt
- 1 teaspoon black pepper
- 1 tablespoon fresh rosemary (chopped)
- 1 cup chicken broth

  Instructions:
1. **Preheat Oven:** Preheat your oven to 325°F (165°C).
2. **Prepare Goose:** Rinse the goose and pat it dry. Rub the skin with olive oil, salt, pepper, and rosemary.
3. **Stuff Goose:** Stuff the cavity with apple quarters and onion.
4. **Roast:** Place the goose breast side up in a roasting pan and pour chicken broth into the pan. Roast for about 3-4 hours, basting every 30 minutes, until the internal temperature reaches 165°F (74°C).
5. **Serve:** Let rest for 15-20 minutes before carving. Serve with roasted apples.

Venison Meatballs in Marinara Sauce
Ingredients:

- 1 pound ground venison
- 1/2 cup breadcrumbs
- 1/4 cup grated Parmesan cheese
- 1 egg
- 2 cloves garlic (minced)
- 1 teaspoon Italian seasoning
- Salt and pepper to taste
- 2 cups marinara sauce

Instructions:

1. **Preheat Oven:** Preheat your oven to 400°F (200°C).
2. **Make Meatballs:** In a bowl, mix ground venison, breadcrumbs, Parmesan, egg, garlic, Italian seasoning, salt, and pepper. Form into meatballs.
3. **Bake:** Place meatballs on a baking sheet and bake for 20 minutes.
4. **Simmer in Sauce:** In a skillet, heat marinara sauce. Add meatballs and simmer for 10 minutes.
5. **Serve:** Serve with spaghetti or in a sub sandwich.

Pheasant Pot Pie
Ingredients:

- 1 cooked pheasant (shredded)
- 2 cups mixed vegetables (carrots, peas, corn)
- 1/4 cup onion (chopped)
- 1/4 cup flour
- 2 cups chicken broth
- 1 cup milk
- 1 teaspoon thyme
- Salt and pepper to taste
- 1 pie crust (top and bottom)

Instructions:

1. **Preheat Oven:** Preheat your oven to 425°F (220°C).
2. **Make Filling:** In a saucepan, sauté onion until soft. Stir in flour, cook for 1 minute, then add broth and milk. Cook until thickened.
3. **Combine Ingredients:** Add shredded pheasant and mixed vegetables; season with thyme, salt, and pepper.
4. **Assemble Pie:** Place the bottom crust in a pie dish, fill with pheasant mixture, and cover with the top crust. Cut slits for steam to escape.
5. **Bake:** Bake for 30-35 minutes until golden brown. Let cool before serving.

Grilled Bison Burgers
Ingredients:

- 1 pound ground bison
- 1 tablespoon Worcestershire sauce
- 1 teaspoon garlic powder
- Salt and pepper to taste
- Burger buns
- Optional toppings: lettuce, tomato, cheese, onion
  Instructions:
1. **Preheat Grill:** Preheat your grill to medium-high heat.
2. **Mix Ingredients:** In a bowl, combine ground bison, Worcestershire sauce, garlic powder, salt, and pepper.
3. **Form Patties:** Shape mixture into burger patties.
4. **Grill Patties:** Grill for about 4-5 minutes per side or until cooked to desired doneness.
5. **Serve:** Serve on buns with your favorite toppings.

Braised Rabbit with Mustard Sauce
Ingredients:

- 1 rabbit (cut into pieces)
- 2 tablespoons olive oil
- 1 onion (sliced)
- 2 cloves garlic (minced)
- 1 cup chicken broth
- 1/4 cup Dijon mustard
- 1 tablespoon fresh thyme (chopped)
- Salt and pepper to taste

Instructions:

1. **Sear Rabbit:** In a large pot, heat olive oil over medium heat. Add rabbit pieces and brown on all sides.
2. **Sauté Vegetables:** Remove rabbit and add onion and garlic to the pot; cook until softened.
3. **Add Liquid:** Return rabbit to pot, add chicken broth, Dijon mustard, thyme, salt, and pepper.
4. **Simmer:** Cover and simmer for about 1.5 to 2 hours until rabbit is tender.
5. **Serve:** Serve warm with sauce spooned over the top.

Wild Game Sausage
Ingredients:

- 2 pounds mixed wild game meat (venison, elk, etc.)
- 1/2 pound pork fat
- 2 tablespoons salt
- 1 tablespoon black pepper
- 1 tablespoon garlic powder
- 1 tablespoon sage
- Sausage casings (if making links)

Instructions:

1. **Grind Meat:** Grind wild game and pork fat together.
2. **Mix Spices:** In a bowl, combine ground meat with salt, pepper, garlic powder, and sage. Mix thoroughly.
3. **Stuff Sausages:** If using casings, stuff mixture into casings and tie off. Otherwise, shape into patties.
4. **Cook:** Grill or pan-fry sausages until cooked through.
5. **Serve:** Serve with your favorite sides or in a sandwich.

Venison Jerky
Ingredients:

- 2 pounds venison (sliced thin)
- 1/4 cup soy sauce
- 1/4 cup Worcestershire sauce
- 1 tablespoon black pepper
- 1 tablespoon garlic powder
- 1 tablespoon onion powder
- 1 teaspoon smoked paprika

Instructions:

1. **Marinate Meat:** In a bowl, mix soy sauce, Worcestershire sauce, black pepper, garlic powder, onion powder, and smoked paprika. Add venison slices and marinate for at least 4 hours or overnight.
2. **Preheat Dehydrator:** If using a dehydrator, preheat to 160°F (70°C).
3. **Dehydrate:** Arrange venison slices on dehydrator trays in a single layer. Dehydrate for 6-8 hours until jerky is dry and flexible.
4. **Cool and Store:** Let cool and store in an airtight container.
5. **Enjoy:** Snack on jerky as a protein-rich treat!

Slow Cooker Wild Game Stew
Ingredients:

- 2 pounds mixed wild game (venison, elk, rabbit, etc.), cut into chunks
- 4 carrots, chopped
- 3 potatoes, diced
- 1 onion, chopped
- 3 cloves garlic, minced
- 4 cups beef or game broth
- 1 tablespoon tomato paste
- 1 teaspoon dried thyme
- 1 teaspoon rosemary
- Salt and pepper to taste
- 1 cup frozen peas

Instructions:

1. **Prepare Ingredients:** In a slow cooker, combine wild game, carrots, potatoes, onion, and garlic.
2. **Add Liquid:** Pour in the broth and add tomato paste, thyme, rosemary, salt, and pepper. Stir to combine.
3. **Cook:** Cover and cook on low for 6-8 hours or until meat is tender.
4. **Add Peas:** In the last 30 minutes of cooking, stir in the frozen peas.
5. **Serve:** Adjust seasoning if needed and serve hot with crusty bread.

Quail with Blackberry Glaze
Ingredients:

- 4 quail, cleaned
- 1 cup fresh blackberries
- 1/4 cup balsamic vinegar
- 2 tablespoons honey
- 1 tablespoon olive oil
- Salt and pepper to taste

Instructions:

1. **Prepare Glaze:** In a saucepan, combine blackberries, balsamic vinegar, honey, olive oil, salt, and pepper. Cook over medium heat until blackberries break down, about 5-7 minutes.
2. **Season Quail:** Season quail with salt and pepper.
3. **Cook Quail:** Preheat grill or skillet over medium heat. Cook quail for about 4-5 minutes per side until cooked through.
4. **Glaze Quail:** Brush blackberry glaze over the quail during the last few minutes of cooking.
5. **Serve:** Serve hot, drizzled with extra glaze.

Elk Fajitas
Ingredients:

- 1 pound elk steak, sliced thin
- 1 bell pepper, sliced
- 1 onion, sliced
- 2 tablespoons olive oil
- 2 teaspoons chili powder
- 1 teaspoon cumin
- Salt and pepper to taste
- Flour or corn tortillas

Instructions:

1. **Cook Vegetables:** In a large skillet, heat olive oil over medium-high heat. Add bell pepper and onion, cooking until softened, about 5 minutes. Remove from skillet and set aside.
2. **Cook Elk:** In the same skillet, add elk steak, chili powder, cumin, salt, and pepper. Cook until meat is browned and cooked to desired doneness.
3. **Combine:** Return the cooked vegetables to the skillet and stir to combine.
4. **Serve:** Serve elk mixture in warmed tortillas with your favorite toppings.

Stuffed Pheasant Breast
Ingredients:

- 4 pheasant breasts
- 1 cup spinach, cooked and chopped
- 1/2 cup cream cheese, softened
- 1/4 cup feta cheese, crumbled
- Salt and pepper to taste
- 1/2 cup breadcrumbs

Instructions:

1. **Prepare Filling:** In a bowl, mix cooked spinach, cream cheese, feta, salt, and pepper.
2. **Stuff Breasts:** Cut a pocket into each pheasant breast and fill with the spinach mixture.
3. **Coat Breasts:** Roll the stuffed breasts in breadcrumbs.
4. **Cook:** Preheat oven to 375°F (190°C). Place stuffed breasts on a baking sheet and bake for 25-30 minutes, or until cooked through.
5. **Serve:** Slice and serve warm.

Wild Mushroom and Venison Risotto

Ingredients:

- 1 pound venison (cut into small pieces)
- 1 cup arborio rice
- 4 cups beef broth
- 1 cup wild mushrooms (sliced)
- 1 onion, chopped
- 2 cloves garlic, minced
- 1/2 cup white wine
- 1/2 cup Parmesan cheese, grated
- 2 tablespoons olive oil
- Salt and pepper to taste
- Fresh parsley for garnish

Instructions:

1. **Cook Venison:** In a skillet, heat olive oil over medium heat. Add venison and cook until browned. Remove and set aside.
2. **Sauté Vegetables:** In the same skillet, add onion and garlic; cook until softened. Add mushrooms and cook for another 3-4 minutes.
3. **Cook Rice:** Stir in arborio rice, cooking for 1-2 minutes. Add white wine and cook until absorbed.
4. **Add Broth:** Gradually add beef broth, one ladle at a time, stirring frequently until rice is creamy and al dente.
5. **Combine:** Stir in cooked venison and Parmesan cheese. Season with salt and pepper. Garnish with parsley before serving.

Herb-Crusted Wild Boar Tenderloin

Ingredients:

- 1 pound wild boar tenderloin
- 2 tablespoons Dijon mustard
- 1/4 cup breadcrumbs
- 2 tablespoons fresh parsley, chopped
- 1 tablespoon fresh rosemary, chopped
- 1 tablespoon olive oil
- Salt and pepper to taste

Instructions:

1. **Preheat Oven:** Preheat your oven to 400°F (200°C).
2. **Prepare Tenderloin:** Season wild boar tenderloin with salt and pepper. Spread Dijon mustard over the surface.
3. **Make Herb Mixture:** In a bowl, mix breadcrumbs, parsley, rosemary, and olive oil.
4. **Coat Tenderloin:** Press the herb mixture onto the mustard-coated tenderloin.
5. **Bake:** Place the tenderloin on a baking sheet and bake for 20-25 minutes or until it reaches an internal temperature of 145°F (63°C).
6. **Serve:** Let rest for 5 minutes before slicing and serving.

Rabbit Cacciatore

Ingredients:

- 1 rabbit, cut into pieces
- 2 tablespoons olive oil
- 1 onion, chopped
- 2 cloves garlic, minced
- 1 bell pepper, chopped
- 1 can (14 oz) diced tomatoes
- 1 cup chicken broth
- 1 tablespoon Italian seasoning
- Salt and pepper to taste
- Fresh parsley for garnish

Instructions:

1. **Sear Rabbit:** In a large skillet, heat olive oil over medium-high heat. Season rabbit pieces with salt and pepper and brown them in the skillet. Remove and set aside.
2. **Sauté Vegetables:** In the same skillet, add onion, garlic, and bell pepper. Cook until softened, about 5 minutes.
3. **Combine Ingredients:** Add diced tomatoes, chicken broth, Italian seasoning, and the browned rabbit back to the skillet.
4. **Simmer:** Cover and simmer for 1-1.5 hours, until the rabbit is tender.
5. **Serve:** Garnish with fresh parsley and serve hot over pasta or polenta.

Grilled Duck Legs with Honey Glaze
Ingredients:

- 4 duck legs
- Salt and pepper to taste
- 1/4 cup honey
- 2 tablespoons soy sauce
- 1 tablespoon Dijon mustard
- 1 tablespoon apple cider vinegar

Instructions:

1. **Prepare Marinade:** In a bowl, whisk together honey, soy sauce, Dijon mustard, apple cider vinegar, salt, and pepper.
2. **Marinate Duck:** Rub the duck legs with salt and pepper, then marinate in the honey mixture for at least 1 hour (or overnight for best results).
3. **Grill Duck:** Preheat grill to medium heat. Grill duck legs for 30-35 minutes, turning occasionally, until cooked through and the skin is crispy.
4. **Serve:** Brush with remaining marinade during grilling and serve hot.

Venison Shepherd's Pie
Ingredients:

- 1 pound ground venison
- 1 onion, chopped
- 2 carrots, diced
- 2 cloves garlic, minced
- 1 cup frozen peas
- 1 tablespoon Worcestershire sauce
- 1 cup beef broth
- 4 cups mashed potatoes
- Salt and pepper to taste
- 1 tablespoon olive oil

Instructions:

1. **Cook Filling:** In a skillet, heat olive oil over medium heat. Add onion and garlic; sauté until softened. Add ground venison and cook until browned. Stir in carrots, peas, Worcestershire sauce, beef broth, salt, and pepper. Cook for another 5 minutes.
2. **Assemble Pie:** Preheat oven to 400°F (200°C). Spread the venison mixture in a baking dish, then top with mashed potatoes, spreading evenly.
3. **Bake:** Bake for 20-25 minutes until the top is golden brown.
4. **Serve:** Let cool for a few minutes before serving.

Pan-Fried Quail with Country Gravy
Ingredients:

- 4 quail, cleaned
- Salt and pepper to taste
- 1 cup buttermilk
- 1 cup flour
- 1 tablespoon paprika
- 2 tablespoons butter
- 2 cups milk
- 1/4 cup chicken broth

Instructions:

1. **Marinate Quail:** Season quail with salt and pepper, then soak in buttermilk for at least 30 minutes.
2. **Prepare Coating:** In a shallow dish, mix flour, paprika, salt, and pepper.
3. **Fry Quail:** Heat butter in a skillet over medium heat. Dredge each quail in the flour mixture and fry until golden brown on all sides. Remove and set aside.
4. **Make Gravy:** In the same skillet, whisk in milk and chicken broth, scraping up any bits from the pan. Cook until thickened, about 5 minutes.
5. **Serve:** Serve the fried quail hot with country gravy.

Wild Game Jambalaya

Ingredients:

- 1 pound mixed wild game (venison, rabbit, etc.), diced
- 1 onion, chopped
- 1 bell pepper, chopped
- 2 celery stalks, chopped
- 3 cloves garlic, minced
- 1 can (14 oz) diced tomatoes
- 2 cups rice
- 4 cups chicken broth
- 2 teaspoons Cajun seasoning
- Salt and pepper to taste
- 2 tablespoons olive oil

Instructions:

1. **Sauté Vegetables:** In a large pot, heat olive oil over medium heat. Add onion, bell pepper, celery, and garlic; sauté until softened.
2. **Add Game:** Stir in wild game and cook until browned.
3. **Combine Ingredients:** Add diced tomatoes, rice, chicken broth, Cajun seasoning, salt, and pepper.
4. **Simmer:** Bring to a boil, then reduce heat to low and cover. Cook for 20-25 minutes until the rice is tender.
5. **Serve:** Fluff with a fork and serve hot.

Bison Meatloaf
Ingredients:

- 1 pound ground bison
- 1 cup breadcrumbs
- 1/2 cup milk
- 1 onion, finely chopped
- 2 cloves garlic, minced
- 1 egg
- 2 tablespoons ketchup
- Salt and pepper to taste

Instructions:

1. **Preheat Oven:** Preheat oven to 350°F (175°C).
2. **Mix Ingredients:** In a bowl, combine ground bison, breadcrumbs, milk, onion, garlic, egg, ketchup, salt, and pepper. Mix until well combined.
3. **Shape Meatloaf:** Transfer the mixture to a loaf pan and shape into a loaf.
4. **Bake:** Bake for 1 hour or until cooked through.
5. **Serve:** Let rest for a few minutes before slicing and serving.

Smoked Venison Tenderloin

Ingredients:

- 1 venison tenderloin
- 2 tablespoons olive oil
- 2 tablespoons smoked paprika
- 1 tablespoon garlic powder
- Salt and pepper to taste
- Wood chips for smoking

Instructions:

1. **Prepare Marinade:** Rub tenderloin with olive oil, smoked paprika, garlic powder, salt, and pepper. Let marinate for at least 1 hour.
2. **Prepare Smoker:** Preheat your smoker to 225°F (107°C). Soak wood chips in water for 30 minutes before using.
3. **Smoke Tenderloin:** Place tenderloin in the smoker and add wood chips. Smoke for about 2-3 hours or until it reaches an internal temperature of 130°F (54°C) for medium-rare.
4. **Rest and Slice:** Let rest for 10 minutes before slicing.
5. **Serve:** Serve sliced, with sides of your choice.

Duck Confit

Ingredients:

- 4 duck legs
- 2 cups duck fat (or olive oil)
- 4 cloves garlic, smashed
- 4 sprigs fresh thyme
- Salt and pepper to taste

Instructions:

1. **Cure Duck Legs:** Season duck legs with salt and pepper. Place in a dish and add garlic and thyme. Cover and refrigerate for at least 24 hours.
2. **Preheat Oven:** Preheat oven to 225°F (110°C).
3. **Cook Duck:** In a large oven-safe pot, melt duck fat over low heat. Add cured duck legs, ensuring they are fully submerged. Cover and cook in the oven for 2-3 hours until tender.
4. **Crisp Skin:** Remove legs from fat and pat dry. Heat a skillet over medium-high heat and sear the skin side until crispy.
5. **Serve:** Serve hot, garnished with fresh herbs.

Elk and Sweet Potato Hash
Ingredients:

- 1 pound ground elk
- 2 medium sweet potatoes, diced
- 1 onion, chopped
- 2 bell peppers, diced
- 2 cloves garlic, minced
- 1 teaspoon paprika
- Salt and pepper to taste
- Olive oil for cooking

Instructions:

1. **Cook Sweet Potatoes:** In a large skillet, heat olive oil over medium heat. Add sweet potatoes and cook until they begin to soften, about 10 minutes.
2. **Add Veggies:** Stir in onion, bell peppers, and garlic. Cook until vegetables are tender.
3. **Cook Elk:** Add ground elk to the skillet, season with paprika, salt, and pepper. Cook until browned and cooked through.
4. **Serve:** Serve hot as a hearty breakfast or dinner option.

Grilled Wild Game Skewers
Ingredients:

- 1 pound mixed wild game (venison, elk, etc.), cut into cubes
- 1 bell pepper, cut into chunks
- 1 onion, cut into chunks
- 2 tablespoons olive oil
- 2 tablespoons soy sauce
- 1 tablespoon garlic powder
- Salt and pepper to taste

Instructions:

1. **Marinate Game:** In a bowl, combine olive oil, soy sauce, garlic powder, salt, and pepper. Add wild game cubes and marinate for at least 1 hour.
2. **Prepare Skewers:** Thread marinated game, bell pepper, and onion onto skewers.
3. **Grill:** Preheat grill to medium-high heat. Grill skewers for 10-12 minutes, turning occasionally, until meat is cooked to desired doneness.
4. **Serve:** Serve hot with your choice of dipping sauce.

Venison and Black Bean Chili

Ingredients:

- 1 pound ground venison
- 1 onion, chopped
- 2 cloves garlic, minced
- 1 can (14 oz) black beans, rinsed and drained
- 1 can (14 oz) diced tomatoes
- 2 cups beef broth
- 1 tablespoon chili powder
- 1 teaspoon cumin
- Salt and pepper to taste

Instructions:

1. **Brown Venison:** In a large pot, cook ground venison over medium heat until browned. Drain excess fat.
2. **Sauté Vegetables:** Add onion and garlic; sauté until softened.
3. **Combine Ingredients:** Stir in black beans, diced tomatoes, beef broth, chili powder, cumin, salt, and pepper.
4. **Simmer:** Bring to a boil, then reduce heat and simmer for 30 minutes.
5. **Serve:** Serve hot with your choice of toppings.

Baked Pheasant with Cranberries
Ingredients:

- 2 pheasants, cleaned
- 1 cup fresh cranberries
- 1 onion, quartered
- 2 tablespoons olive oil
- Salt and pepper to taste
- Fresh rosemary for garnish

Instructions:

1. **Preheat Oven:** Preheat oven to 375°F (190°C).
2. **Prepare Pheasants:** Place pheasants in a roasting pan. Rub with olive oil, salt, and pepper.
3. **Add Cranberries and Onion:** Scatter cranberries and onion around the pheasants.
4. **Bake:** Cover with foil and bake for 45 minutes. Remove foil and bake for an additional 15 minutes until the skin is golden brown.
5. **Serve:** Serve garnished with fresh rosemary.

Rabbit Fricassée

Ingredients:

- 1 rabbit, cut into pieces
- 2 tablespoons butter
- 1 onion, chopped
- 2 carrots, sliced
- 2 cups chicken broth
- 1 cup white wine
- 1 tablespoon fresh thyme
- Salt and pepper to taste

Instructions:

1. **Brown Rabbit:** In a large pot, melt butter over medium heat. Add rabbit pieces and brown on all sides.
2. **Sauté Vegetables:** Add onion and carrots; sauté until softened.
3. **Add Liquids:** Pour in chicken broth and white wine. Stir in thyme, salt, and pepper.
4. **Simmer:** Cover and simmer for about 1 hour until rabbit is tender.
5. **Serve:** Serve hot with crusty bread or over rice.

Wild Turkey Breast with Sage Butter
Ingredients:

- 1 wild turkey breast
- 4 tablespoons butter, softened
- 2 tablespoons fresh sage, chopped
- Salt and pepper to taste

Instructions:

1. **Prepare Sage Butter:** In a bowl, mix softened butter with chopped sage, salt, and pepper.
2. **Prepare Turkey Breast:** Preheat oven to 350°F (175°C). Season turkey breast with salt and pepper.
3. **Roast Turkey:** Place turkey in a roasting pan and spread sage butter over the top. Roast for 1-1.5 hours, until the internal temperature reaches 165°F (74°C).
4. **Serve:** Let rest for 10 minutes before slicing. Serve hot with your favorite sides.

Venison Stroganoff with Egg Noodles

Ingredients:

- 1 pound venison, thinly sliced
- 8 ounces egg noodles
- 1 onion, chopped
- 2 cloves garlic, minced
- 1 cup mushrooms, sliced
- 1 cup beef broth
- 1 cup sour cream
- 2 tablespoons flour
- 2 tablespoons olive oil
- Salt and pepper to taste

Instructions:

1. **Cook Noodles:** Cook egg noodles according to package instructions; drain and set aside.
2. **Sauté Meat:** In a large skillet, heat olive oil over medium-high heat. Add venison and cook until browned. Remove and set aside.
3. **Sauté Vegetables:** In the same skillet, add onion, garlic, and mushrooms. Cook until softened.
4. **Make Sauce:** Sprinkle flour over vegetables, stirring well. Slowly add beef broth, bring to a simmer, and stir until thickened.
5. **Combine:** Return venison to the skillet, stir in sour cream, and heat through. Serve over egg noodles.

Grilled Bison Steak with Chimichurri

Ingredients:

- 2 bison steaks
- Salt and pepper to taste
- 1/2 cup fresh parsley, chopped
- 1/4 cup olive oil
- 2 tablespoons red wine vinegar
- 2 cloves garlic, minced
- 1 teaspoon red pepper flakes

Instructions:

1. **Prepare Chimichurri:** In a bowl, mix parsley, olive oil, red wine vinegar, garlic, and red pepper flakes. Set aside.
2. **Season Steaks:** Preheat grill to medium-high heat. Season bison steaks with salt and pepper.
3. **Grill Steaks:** Grill steaks for about 4-5 minutes per side for medium-rare, or until desired doneness.
4. **Serve:** Let rest for a few minutes, then slice and serve with chimichurri sauce.

Roasted Wild Duck with Orange Sauce

Ingredients:

- 2 wild ducks, cleaned
- 1 cup orange juice
- 1/2 cup chicken broth
- 2 tablespoons honey
- 1 tablespoon soy sauce
- 2 oranges, sliced
- Salt and pepper to taste

Instructions:

1. **Preheat Oven:** Preheat oven to 375°F (190°C).
2. **Prepare Duck:** Season ducks with salt and pepper. Place in a roasting pan and surround with orange slices.
3. **Make Sauce:** In a bowl, mix orange juice, chicken broth, honey, and soy sauce. Pour over ducks.
4. **Roast Duck:** Roast for 1-1.5 hours, basting occasionally, until cooked through and juices run clear.
5. **Serve:** Serve hot with orange sauce drizzled over.

Venison Fajitas with Peppers
Ingredients:

- 1 pound venison, sliced into strips
- 1 bell pepper, sliced
- 1 onion, sliced
- 2 tablespoons fajita seasoning
- 2 tablespoons olive oil
- Tortillas for serving

Instructions:

1. **Sauté Vegetables:** In a skillet, heat olive oil over medium heat. Add onion and bell pepper; sauté until softened. Remove from skillet and set aside.
2. **Cook Venison:** In the same skillet, add venison and fajita seasoning. Cook until venison is browned and cooked through.
3. **Combine:** Add the sautéed vegetables back to the skillet and mix well.
4. **Serve:** Serve hot in tortillas with your choice of toppings.

Spicy Wild Boar Chili

Ingredients:

- 1 pound ground wild boar
- 1 onion, chopped
- 2 cloves garlic, minced
- 1 can (14 oz) diced tomatoes
- 1 can (14 oz) kidney beans, drained
- 2 tablespoons chili powder
- 1 teaspoon cumin
- 1 teaspoon cayenne pepper
- Salt and pepper to taste

Instructions:

1. **Cook Boar:** In a large pot, brown the ground wild boar over medium heat. Drain excess fat.
2. **Sauté Vegetables:** Add onion and garlic; sauté until softened.
3. **Combine Ingredients:** Stir in diced tomatoes, kidney beans, chili powder, cumin, cayenne pepper, salt, and pepper.
4. **Simmer:** Bring to a boil, then reduce heat and simmer for 30 minutes.
5. **Serve:** Serve hot with cornbread or over rice.

Braised Elk Shanks
Ingredients:

- 2 elk shanks
- 1 onion, chopped
- 2 carrots, chopped
- 2 celery stalks, chopped
- 4 cloves garlic, minced
- 2 cups beef broth
- 1 cup red wine
- 2 sprigs fresh thyme
- Salt and pepper to taste

Instructions:

1. **Sear Elk:** In a large pot, heat oil over medium-high heat. Season elk shanks with salt and pepper, and brown on all sides.
2. **Add Vegetables:** Remove elk shanks and set aside. In the same pot, add onion, carrots, celery, and garlic; sauté until softened.
3. **Add Liquids:** Return elk shanks to the pot. Add beef broth, red wine, and thyme.
4. **Braise:** Cover and simmer on low for 2-3 hours until meat is tender.
5. **Serve:** Serve hot with mashed potatoes or crusty bread.

Pheasant Enchiladas
Ingredients:

- 2 cups cooked pheasant, shredded
- 8 corn tortillas
- 1 cup enchilada sauce
- 1 cup cheese (cheddar or Monterey Jack)
- 1 onion, chopped
- 1 bell pepper, chopped
- Olive oil for sautéing

Instructions:

1. **Preheat Oven:** Preheat oven to 350°F (175°C).
2. **Sauté Vegetables:** In a skillet, heat olive oil over medium heat. Add onion and bell pepper; sauté until softened.
3. **Fill Tortillas:** On each tortilla, place shredded pheasant and sautéed vegetables. Roll up and place seam-side down in a baking dish.
4. **Add Sauce and Cheese:** Pour enchilada sauce over the top and sprinkle with cheese.
5. **Bake:** Bake for 20-25 minutes until heated through and cheese is bubbly. Serve hot.

Duck Breast with Cherry Sauce
Ingredients:

- 2 duck breasts
- Salt and pepper to taste
- 1 cup fresh or frozen cherries
- 1/2 cup red wine
- 2 tablespoons honey
- 1 tablespoon balsamic vinegar
- 1 tablespoon butter

Instructions:

1. **Prepare Duck:** Score the skin of the duck breasts and season with salt and pepper.
2. **Sear Duck:** In a skillet, place the duck breasts skin-side down over medium heat. Cook until the skin is crispy, about 6-8 minutes. Flip and cook for an additional 3-4 minutes.
3. **Make Sauce:** Remove the duck and let it rest. In the same skillet, add cherries, red wine, honey, and balsamic vinegar. Cook until reduced by half. Stir in butter until melted and smooth.
4. **Serve:** Slice duck breasts and serve with cherry sauce drizzled on top.

Venison Ragu with Pasta
Ingredients:

- 1 pound ground venison
- 1 onion, chopped
- 2 cloves garlic, minced
- 1 carrot, diced
- 1 celery stalk, diced
- 1 can (14 oz) crushed tomatoes
- 1 cup red wine
- 1 teaspoon Italian seasoning
- Salt and pepper to taste
- Pasta of choice

Instructions:

1. **Cook Pasta:** Cook pasta according to package instructions; drain and set aside.
2. **Sauté Vegetables:** In a large skillet, heat olive oil over medium heat. Add onion, garlic, carrot, and celery; sauté until softened.
3. **Brown Venison:** Add ground venison and cook until browned.
4. **Add Sauce Ingredients:** Stir in crushed tomatoes, red wine, Italian seasoning, salt, and pepper. Simmer for 30 minutes.
5. **Combine:** Toss the ragu with the cooked pasta and serve hot.

Grilled Quail with Lemon and Thyme
Ingredients:

- 4 quail, cleaned
- Salt and pepper to taste
- 2 lemons, juiced and zested
- 2 tablespoons fresh thyme, chopped
- Olive oil for brushing

Instructions:

1. **Marinate Quail:** In a bowl, combine lemon juice, zest, thyme, salt, and pepper. Add quail and marinate for at least 30 minutes.
2. **Preheat Grill:** Preheat grill to medium-high heat.
3. **Grill Quail:** Remove quail from marinade and brush with olive oil. Grill for about 4-5 minutes per side until cooked through.
4. **Serve:** Serve warm with lemon wedges.

Elk Meatballs with Cranberry Sauce

Ingredients:

- 1 pound ground elk
- 1/2 cup breadcrumbs
- 1/4 cup grated Parmesan cheese
- 1 egg
- 2 cloves garlic, minced
- Salt and pepper to taste
- 1 cup cranberry sauce (store-bought or homemade)

Instructions:

1. **Preheat Oven:** Preheat oven to 400°F (200°C).
2. **Mix Meatball Ingredients:** In a bowl, combine ground elk, breadcrumbs, Parmesan, egg, garlic, salt, and pepper. Mix until well combined.
3. **Form Meatballs:** Shape mixture into meatballs and place on a baking sheet.
4. **Bake:** Bake for 20-25 minutes until cooked through.
5. **Serve:** Serve warm with cranberry sauce drizzled on top.

Stuffed Rabbit Loin
Ingredients:

- 1 rabbit loin, butterflied
- 1/2 cup spinach, chopped
- 1/4 cup feta cheese, crumbled
- 1/4 cup sun-dried tomatoes, chopped
- Salt and pepper to taste
- Olive oil for drizzling

Instructions:

1. **Preheat Oven:** Preheat oven to 375°F (190°C).
2. **Prepare Filling:** In a bowl, mix spinach, feta, sun-dried tomatoes, salt, and pepper.
3. **Stuff Loin:** Spread filling over the butterflied rabbit loin and roll it up. Secure with toothpicks.
4. **Bake:** Place on a baking sheet, drizzle with olive oil, and bake for 25-30 minutes until cooked through.
5. **Serve:** Slice and serve hot.

Wild Game Curry
Ingredients:

- 1 pound diced wild game (venison, elk, etc.)
- 1 onion, chopped
- 2 cloves garlic, minced
- 1 tablespoon ginger, grated
- 2 tablespoons curry powder
- 1 can (14 oz) coconut milk
- 2 cups vegetables (carrots, bell peppers, etc.)
- Salt to taste

Instructions:

1. **Sauté Aromatics:** In a pot, heat oil over medium heat. Add onion, garlic, and ginger; sauté until softened.
2. **Brown Game:** Add diced wild game and cook until browned.
3. **Add Curry Powder:** Stir in curry powder and cook for another minute.
4. **Add Coconut Milk and Veggies:** Pour in coconut milk and add vegetables. Simmer for 30 minutes until the meat is tender.
5. **Serve:** Serve hot over rice or with naan.